High Impact Ideas
For Your Life

High Impact Ideas
For Your Life

Become the "you" you were meant to be.

Conceive   Believe

Inspire

Achieve

By

Carl F. Hicks, Jr., Ph.D.

ISBN: 0615929222
ISBN-13: 978-0615929224
Library of Congress Control Number: 2013922476

High Impact Publishing, Chevy Chase, Maryland
www.HighImpactPublishing.com

Printed in the United States of America

*For Tommy, Natalya, and Mahmoud.
Each in their own way has changed
my worldview and my life . . .
for the better.*

Acknowledgements

An endeavor such as this is never the result of individual effort, so this book has many 'authors'.

To all the people I have had the pleasure of working with, I thank you for the lessons learned.

To my grandmothers, Delphine Goetz Hicks and Eloise Salvo Evans, who patiently listened and instinctively knew when to ask a life-changing question like "Are you happy?" - a question that influenced me to leave a successful career in my mid-thirties and pursue my true calling.

To my father, Carl Franklin Hicks, Sr., who taught me, "No matter where you are or what you are doing, some degree of excellence is within your reach."

To my mother, Marjorie Evans Hicks, who always assured me that "everything would be better in the morning."

To my wife, Carolyn, who believed in my vision of what I could do, who I could become, and never ceased to support my dreams—all of them.

To my cousin, Bill Voss, who taught me the value of vividly imagining and enthusiastically pursuing worthwhile goals.

To my teacher and mentor, S. Roland Jones, Ph.D., who stressed the importance of decisiveness and clarity of direction by challenging me with one simple question: "What do you want to do?"

To my literary sisters, Heather Curtis and Karen Kerley, who magically and easily distinguish between the right word and the almost right word every time.

And to Josh, who keeps suggesting themes and topics.

Table of Contents

Table of Contents

Introduction

Are you living the life you were meant to live? Are you actively pursuing the ideas and dreams that excite you, that give your life meaning and purpose? Are you using the interesting blend of talents and qualities that make you *you*?

With *High Impact Ideas For Your Life* be inspired to act with greater purpose, to create an authentic, meaningful life using the talents, skills and passions that make you unique. A collection of thoughts and observations, *High Impact Ideas For Your Life* is intended to help you reach your full potential with these four steps:

- **Conceive** in your mind your future reality. See and feel your enjoyment.

- **Believe** that this future is possible for you. You deserve the best.

- **Achieve** your future by ardently pursuing your goals. Enjoy the journey.

- **Inspire** others by realizing your full potential. Share your finest moment.

It's never too late to make your dreams a reality or to become the person you were meant to be. Start today!

Conceive

Conceive

Believe

Inspire

Achieve

All personal growth begins with a mental picture of what is possible. Dream big! Visualize how you will feel when your dreams for your future become your reality. Hold tight to your vision. Start *being* today what you visualize for all of your tomorrows.

Room for Growth

Daily life is busy. Between the responsibilities of career and family, it can be a happy, chaotic blur of activity that makes constant demands of our time and energy. And in this hectic, busy life, the idea of thinking bigger and pushing limits can seem almost absurd.

Yet, how often does a lack of time, money, or energy simply become an excuse to settle into a state of comfortable stagnation?

It's wonderful to be satisfied with the state of your life, to be content, but there is always room for growth. It may require some reorganization, perhaps even a few sacrifices. But isn't it worth the time and effort in order to accomplish something greater?

Perhaps it's a dream not realized or a talent not yet honed. Maybe there are goals, either personal or professional, that you've yet to meet but would very much like to. Or perhaps you've been feeling a certain dissatisfaction with the life you are currently living. Whatever the case, there is always room in your life for challenge and growth.

It is only when you are willing to *think bigger, push limits,* and *imagine the impossible* that you are able to become the truest, fullest, and greatest version of yourself - the person you were meant to be.

A Hidden Talent is a Wasted Talent

A talent is a funny thing. It sometimes rears its head early in life - sometimes much later. It may even go undiscovered. But what a terrible shame if it's hidden!

Too often we are the greatest critics of our own talents. We're too quick to decide they aren't good enough or that they have little value. So we keep them to ourselves.

But a talent, no matter how great or how small, is an essential part of who and what you are.

Human beings are made up of a wonderfully unique blend of qualities and attributes - lots of interesting parts that make up the whole. A talent is one of these parts. To ignore it, push it aside, or hide it will only lead to feelings of dissatisfaction and unfulfilled potential because it is an important piece of who you are.

Talents have purpose. They were given to you for a reason. Finding and using your talents will certainly bring a sense of joy and self-fulfillment, but they may also have a positive impact on the world around you. Your talents can be used to help others.

So find your talents, use your talents, and never hide them - because they have the potential to do great good in your life and in the lives of others.

Do What You Love, Love What You Do

For many, a job is simply a means to a paycheck. They show up, "punch the clock", do the work required, go home, and do it all again the next day. The paycheck at the end of the week is the only rewarding part of the job - the only incentive to show up everyday.

There's certainly nothing wrong with working to earn a living. After all, a paycheck provides for life's necessities: food, clothes, and a roof overhead. But how much more fulfilling and satisfying it is to spend your time and energy doing something you enjoy!

Finding a way to earn a living doing something you actually want to do everyday should be a top priority in life. The time spent working is more than an investment of your time and energy. It is an investment of your life.

Find a way to combine your interests and abilities with activities that serve others, and suddenly what you do for a living may become more than a job. It may become a *calling*.

Do what you love, *love* what you do, and you'll never really *work* a day in your life!

There is Only One Authentic You

It's not unusual for something of value to come with a Certificate of Authenticity. Whether it's for a beautiful piece of artwork, notable memorabilia, or a precious stone, the Certificate is documented proof that the item is exactly what it claims to be - that it is genuine.

As valuable as they are, our lives come with no such documentation. But if they did, is the life you're living now worthy of a Certificate of Authenticity?

Who is the authentic you?

Quite simply, the authentic you is the *you* that you were born to be. All the talents, the passions, the interests, the quirks, and the traits wrapped up into one unique individual and then utilized, put into action, and lived out for all to see. It is the most honest and sincere version of you - the fullest, happiest version of you.

By living anything less than the *authentic* you, you run the risk of never reaching your full potential. Everything from job satisfaction to personal relationships suffer because the real you, the *authentic* you, is not fully engaged or fully committed.

There is only one authentic you. *Find* who you truly are; *live* who you truly are.

Meant to Be

Ask any child the simple question, "What do you want to be when you grow up," and you'll usually get a quick, confident answer: firefighter, doctor, astronaut, chef, athlete, and so on. The same question, however, is not as simple when you've already "grown up," and it can be much harder to answer.

For a "grown up," the question feels more personal, more urgent. "What do I want to be right now?" It may even take on greater weight. "What am I supposed to be doing with my life right now?"

We all know life is short. It's too short to waste, and it's too precious to live feeling dissatisfied, unfulfilled, or uncertain with choices made or unmade.

It's never too late to become what you might have been or what you were meant to be.

Start becoming the person you were meant to be by embracing the things that make you *you*. Explore your talents and gifts; hone skills that may have gone undeveloped or even unnoticed. Have confidence that all the qualities, the gifts, the passions, and interests that you possess are not random or unnecessary, but purposeful. They shape the person you are and the person you are supposed to be.

Do You Know Your *WHY*?

Most people have a ready reply when asked, "What do you do for a living?" Some have their thirty-second "elevator speech" down pat. They're quite clear about their *WHAT*.

But, if you ask them *WHY* they do what they do, you might get a hesitant response - if one at all.

How would you respond if someone were to ask you, "*Why do you do what you do?*" The *WHY* question doesn't often generate a rapid response.

Perhaps it's because we're rarely asked this question. Or, could it be because we simply haven't thought about it very deeply? You may be wondering why the *WHY* question and someone's response to it even matter?

It matters because a person's *WHY* determines *HOW* they are *WHO* they are.

Do you know your *WHY*?

Why Being Your Best Is Best For You

When you align your performance with your potential, it shows the world that you are in touch with your talents, that you respect yourself, and that you want to do your best to be the best you can be.

In short, you show the world that you want to be your authentic self. Why would you want to settle for less? Why would you want to show the world anything else?

No matter where you are or what you're doing, some degree of excellence is within your reach.

Be a DAY Dreamer

What is a dream never pursued? How about an idea never brought to fruition, a talent never explored, or a story never told? The answer is simple: useless.

It's a special kind of blessing to be given an idea, a dream. But without action, such a blessing is wasted. It will never see the light of day; it will never become a reality.

A DAY dreamer, however, understands that a dream is not something to be ignored or wasted. It's the beginning of something great.

Make your dream a DAY dream:

1. **D**evelop the dream: cultivate the dream so that it is a definable, relatable idea that can become an achievable reality.
2. **A**pply a plan: establish a goal-oriented plan to bring the idea to life.
3. **Y**ield results: put the plan into action.

Be a DAY dreamer. Act on your dream, and make it a reality!!

Questions to Consider

1. What makes you happy? What brings you joy? What is your *WHY*?

2. Do you have a clear picture of your *Life Style Goals*? Are there areas of your life that you want to focus on more? How balanced is your life?

3. Are your *Livelihood Goals* in alignment with your *Life Style Goals*?

Believe

Conceive   **Believe**

Inspire

Achieve

Confidence is critical. Passionately believe that the future you conceived is attainable. *You* control the ideas, fears, and opportunities that enter your mind. *Positive* thinking is important, and so is *possibility* thinking. On the road to your future, stay focused on the beliefs that enable success.

How You Think is Everything

Regardless of how you define success, it does not happen on its own. Whether you seek enhanced wealth, health, relationships, intellectual insight, spiritual growth, or service to others, it is important to understand what is involved. Achieving success requires clear thinking, an enabling belief system, and purposeful behavior.

Is your worldview large enough to encompass your dreams? The type of thinking that helped you get to where you are today may not be sufficient to take you to the next level of success you desire. Challenge your assumptions. Does your belief system reflect an *abundance* mentality or a *scarcity* mentality?

Do you have a compelling reason to pursue your dreams?

Do you sincerely believe you can reach your desired future?

Can you imagine being there now?

Are you willing to go the distance?

How you think is everything, and everything depends upon the depth of your belief system.

Determination

Goals provide a focal point in the future for our journeys. They can serve as a beacon providing illumination.

But we all know some journeys can be difficult. They can become stressful. We can become tired. And, we can start to question the continuing relevance of our pursuits. What should we do?

It is at times like these that we may need to reach deep inside our belief system to find the determination and will to press on. Reaffirm your belief in yourself and in your future.

Perhaps you're feeling overwhelmed by the size of your goals. If so, try dividing your goals into "bite-size" chunks to make them more manageable.

Re-examine how realistic your time frames are, and, if possible, cut yourself some slack. Would you be happier reaching your destination a little late or not at all?

Reflect on the quantity of goals you are currently pursuing. How many are realistic for you? Learn to say *no* and be careful of overcommitting.

Then, try visualizing how good you'll feel when you finally do arrive at your destination. Find renewed energy in taking one thing at a time. Each step really does add up!

In Peru there is a saying that "little by little one walks far." Believe that each step, no matter how small, does count!

Be Yourself

As a kid, it wasn't unusual to want to be someone else - Johnny the football star, Sarah the math whiz, Peter the artist. We spent more than a passing thought wondering what it would be like to be them.

Now, older and wiser, we don't necessarily look at someone else's life and wish it were our own. We don't want to be someone else.

Yet, we don't always appreciate the person we see in the mirror.

There is only one you. Believe in your greatness. No one else has the exact blend of gifts, talents, emotions, thoughts, and characteristics that you do. By embracing the combination of attributes that make you unique, you'll not only learn to appreciate the person you are, you'll be excited by the person you could be. Cultivate talents, hone skills, grow ideas, and strive to be the best *you* you can be. Anything else is simply a mediocre imitation of someone else.

Be you. No one else can do it quite as well.

Be yourself. Everyone else is already taken!

A Blessing in Disguise

Where there is hope, there is disappointment lurking in the shadows waiting to pounce. At least, it often seems that way. We've all experienced that hopeful anticipation, the expectation of something promising, only to feel the ache of disappointment.

Whether it's something we've worked hard to accomplish, a reward we expected, or a blessing hoped for, when it doesn't happen, doesn't work, doesn't come, the disappointment can be crushing.

But there are times when a disappointment is actually a blessing in disguise.

Disappointments often present opportunities; they may just be hidden very well behind the disillusionment and frustration. You have to look for them. Be open to thinking outside the box, maybe even willing to move in a different direction - figuratively . . . or literally!

When struck with the blow of disappointment, learn to seek the opportunity. You may just find that the disappointment was simply a blessing in disguise.

The Choice of Happiness

We've all met people who just seem to exude happiness. It's in the happy tune they whistle, the constant smile on their face, or the skip in their step. They seem unaffected by the day-to-day worries or frustrations that burden the rest of us. We admire "happy people." But aren't we also slightly puzzled by them?

Many times we think of "happy people" as natural optimists that were born to be happy. We think of their happiness as nothing more than genetics, like having brown hair or blue eyes. Or maybe we think happiness is situational. When good things happen, we're happy; when bad things happen, we're not. We tell ourselves that "happy people" must be happy because nothing bad is happening to them.

It's easy to dismiss happiness as something out of our control. Yet, the truth is, happiness is not a trait, and it does not have to be dependent on circumstance. Happiness is a choice.

You can *choose* to be happy. Happiness is not a mood or feeling like a passing sense of pleasure or burst of joy. It is a consistent choice to enjoy life in spite of the anxieties and difficulties. Happiness is a decision.

Don't Regret your Regrets

No one would try to drive a car forward by looking in the rearview mirror. Yet sometimes that's how we live our lives - looking backward.

Regretting past decisions or missed opportunities is not only a waste of time, energy, and emotion, it prevents us from enjoying our present, and, more importantly, investing in our future. The past has already happened; it can't be undone or changed. But the future is open and rife with possibility.

Don't miss future opportunities by looking backward rather than forward.

The best is yet to come!

The Inner Light

It's amazing how even the smallest of flames will cast light no matter how thick the darkness surrounding it. A single candle may not light up an entire room, but it will shed enough light to dispel some of the darkness. And sometimes on a black, moonless night, when the darkness closes in, a single flicker of candlelight can make all the difference.

It's often the same for the light from within.

There are always times of darkness in life, times of trial and fear, times that test the resolve or wound the spirit. But it is in these times of darkness that the light from within casts its glow, and the true beauty of one's life - the beauty of hope, joy, and love - is revealed.

The light from within shines brightest in the darkness, and it not only reveals one's true beauty, it reveals one's true *beliefs*.

The Unexpected Gift

John came home one day and was surprised to find a box by his front door. It was wrapped in brown paper and tied with wire. As he lifted it to carry it inside, he winced. The wrapping was abrasive, scratching and scraping his fingertips. Frowning, he placed the box on his kitchen table and began to pull the wire free only to feel another stab of pain as it cut into his finger.

He set to work with the paper, flinching as it continued to abrade his skin. Discarding the wrapping, he looked at the box and gingerly opened the lid. His breath caught as he stared at the pink slip inside.

There are times in life when we're given an unexpected, painful blow. Whether it's professional, such as John's pink slip, or something more personal, the resulting pain, disillusionment, and fear can feel overwhelming.

And yet, it sometimes takes an unexpected setback, as painful as it may be, to push life in a new direction. It is often in these times of crisis that an opportunity presents itself: a shift in focus, a change in perspective, or maybe something even greater - a second chance, a new beginning.

The unexpected 'box' that cuts and scrapes may just turn out to be an unexpected *gift*.

Questions to Consider

1. How strong is your belief system? How deeply do you believe in yourself, in your goals, and in your abilities to grow?

2. Is your worldview one of *abundance* or *scarcity*?

3. Do you believe happiness is a choice you can make?

Achieve

Conceive   Believe

Inspire

Achieve

Achievement creates the reality you've conceived, the reality in which you've believed. While goals and plans are important, action is what propels you. Execution converts goals into reality, gives momentum to your plans, and enables you to live the life you desire.

Action Produces Results

Imagine for a moment that you're going bowling. You know the objective of the game - to roll the bowling ball down the lane and try to knock down as many pins as possible - and you have the proper equipment - the shoes and the ball. You're excited; you enjoy the game. But knowledge and desire are not enough at this point. Now it's time to step into position and send the ball down the lane. Action is required.

You may want to bowl, and you may know how to bowl, but until you apply that knowledge and desire and act upon it, no amount of hoping and wishing will knock over those pins.

It is action that produces results.

Action makes a desired result possible; it transforms ideas into the tangible. The application of knowledge, the use of skills, and the investment of time and energy have the ability to breathe life into a dream and make it a reality.

Have an idea? A wish? A dream? Act!

Failure Isn't an End - Just a Setback

There are few things in life as disheartening as failure. It's not simply the lack of success that stings, it's the disappointment, the frustration of all the time, the energy, the effort seemingly wasted. And that's to say nothing of the potential embarrassment.

But failure does not have to be final. It's merely a bump in the road - an opportunity to see it for what it really is.

Our reaction to failure determines the real outcome. When we treat a failure as a setback as opposed to a conclusion, we are able to continue the journey towards success, perhaps down a different road. Failure can prompt a renewed effort. The occurrence of failure provides an opportunity to step back and take a broader view of the situation. It may also prompt a shift in direction, a change in perspective, and the opening of a door to a far greater opportunity.

Success is a journey. Failure doesn't end the journey, it just makes life more interesting.

Change Enables Growth

Just when life gets good, it changes. We finally find a comfortable spot, an easy, happy routine, or find a certain level of satisfaction, and Life throws us a curve ball. Maybe it's only a mild interruption, or maybe it's a major disruption that threatens all that is stable and familiar. Regardless of the size, weight, or depth of the change, the impact is usually just as unsettling. If things can change without notice, how can we ever hope to build a life that can withstand the shakes and tremors that come our way?

The truth? We can't. But then, life is not about building, it's about growing.

Try to *build* a life, and it will be like building a wooden house on shaky ground. When the tremble of change shakes, the house will fall. But *grow* a life, and it will be like a tree rooted securely in the ground, reaching towards the sky. Change then, like the seasons, becomes part of the growth process.

Change is not a threat, but rather an opportunity for growth. In fact, it is necessary for growth. Change may rattle and shake us, and a few leaves may fall, but it becomes an opportunity to learn and develop, to become stronger, to become wiser.

Grow through the changes that come your way!

Growth in the Downs of Life

Life is full of ups and downs. We enjoy the *ups*. Whether anticipated or unexpected, these are the moments that bring us happiness and satisfaction. The *ups* remind us that life is good.

Life's *downs*, on the other hand, are times of confusion, pain, and sorrow. It's easy to become angry or disillusioned when Life takes an unexpected turn, and we may find ourselves asking, "Why is this happening to me?" or "What have I done to deserve this?"

But perhaps it's in these moments of disappointment that we should learn to ask, "How can I grow from this?"

Personal growth rarely happens on Life's mountaintops, but it blooms and thrives in the rich, dark soil of the valleys. If we can learn to see the *downs* as an opportunity to grow in strength, in wisdom, and in spirit, as painful as the process may be, then we learn not to be defeated by the *downs* but rather find value in them.

We may learn to look *up* in the midst of the rainfall and find the rainbow we couldn't have seen before.

What Lies Within

Life is often compared to a journey - and for very good reason. Like a journey, life stretches out both behind and before us, a path full of twists and turns, mountains and valleys, rocky ground and soft soil.

But if life is like a journey, how often is our focus on the road?

Too often our concern is on the road behind or the road ahead - the past and the future. Whether pleasant or painful, the road behind is just that, behind. While it served to shape and inform, it does not define the present, and it doesn't decide the future. The road ahead is unseen, unknown, waiting to be explored.

The journey's progress and outcome depends on you. The decisions made, the paths chosen, the steps taken are all determined by what lies within not what lies ahead or behind.

Grow from the journey. Learn from the journey. And, above all, enjoy the journey.

Where it began and where it ends will never be as important as how it was made.

The Busyness of Life

Ever caught yourself saying, "There just aren't enough hours in the day?" Or how about, "I'll sleep when I'm dead?" You probably have. We all have.

Somewhere along the way life becomes so full of things to do and places to be that we can barely keep up. And the hours in the day seem to become shorter and shorter making it impossible to get it all done.

Sometimes, however, busyness is just busyness.

Staying busy is not always a sign of productivity. In fact, some activity can simply be a waste of time and energy. And time is precious; it should be spent wisely.

Invest your time in the things that will yield real, meaningful results - things that matter. Set priorities.

What are the things in your life that matter most? Are you investing in them, or are you too *busy*? Learn to say *no* to time- and energy-consumers that don't align with your priorities.

Avoid the *emptiness* of *busyness*. In the end, it won't matter near as much how you *spent* your time, but rather how you *invested* it.

Life's Detours

At the time, it was a major disappointment. The goal I had been pursuing looked to be out of reach. Like a closed road, I had to take a detour. Later I came to learn that we all need detours from time to time.

At a minimum, detours allow us to slow down and re-evaluate those activities and goals that are really important to us and for us. A detour is a temporary change in course that allows us to get back on track, but not necessarily at the same pace we had been going. This "slowing down" gives us an opportunity to think about where we've been, where we're going, and, most importantly, why we're taking that path.

Detours are usually viewed as inconveniences, but they might just be what we need to get back on course.

Being challenged in life is inevitable. Being defeated is optional.

The End Result May Surprise You

There is nothing quite as fulfilling as achieving a goal you've set for yourself. Whether it's something as simple as losing five pounds or something far more difficult like running a marathon, there is a certain satisfaction in the accomplishment.

But is the achievement itself the only reward? Or is the accomplishment of the goal the only result?

No. What you *become* by achieving your goals can often be the greatest accomplishment.

Working towards a goal requires commitment. It requires perseverance, a willingness to learn and improve, a dash of humility, a pinch of patience, and a heaping side of determination.

It is the establishment and pursuit of the goal that builds strength and character. In other words, you become a better person for making the journey, not simply by arriving at the destination.

Questions to Consider

1. Are you acting on your dreams?

2. Are you moving forward despite obstacles?

3. Are you taking steps to accumulate your 10,000 hours of greatness?

Inspire

Conceive   Believe

Inspire

Achieve

Reaching and enjoying your full potential can be a source of inspiration to others. Never underestimate the impact your life will have on others. Being your best can help others unleash *their* greatness.

Positive Impact

As you go about your daily life, are you having a positive impact on others?

Does it make a difference to them that you spoke to them, acknowledged their helpfulness, recognized their strengths, honored their thoughts, valued their presence?

Do they feel better for having interacted with you?

Have you inspired them to become all they're capable of becoming?

Have you made a difference in their day? In their life?

Getting the World Right!

The multi-tasking mother of two young children was trying to meet a project deadline from her home office. No amount of adult reasoning with the two youngsters was having an impact. She needed just fifteen uninterrupted minutes. Suddenly an idea occurred to her. She recalled seeing a picture of the world in a magazine on her desk. She located the page, tore it out of the magazine, and cut it into puzzle size pieces.

Taking some scotch tape, she spread the pieces on the floor and urged her children to "put the world" together. They eagerly pounced on the challenge.

Just as she finished her project, the children exclaimed with glee, "We're finished!"

The mother was surprised at how quickly they accomplished the task and noticed that the picture of the world had no tape showing. Astounded, she asked how they had put the puzzle together. "Easy," one of the children replied. "On the back of the picture of the world was a picture of a smiling person. We knew if we got the person right, the world would be right!"

Sometimes getting the *world* right is as simple as getting the *person* right.

The Content of Character

It's often the simple, everyday choices that have the greatest impact on our lives. The body weakens if poor food choices are made, but can strengthen and thrive with the right daily decisions. Small, daily choices to eat well and stay active can, over time, strengthen the body and keep it healthy.

The positive choices we make produce positive results.

Our character is shaped much the same way - small, daily choices will grow and strengthen the content of our character.

Honesty, responsibility, kindness, courage, fairness, wisdom - these are the qualities of a healthy, well-developed character; these are the *content of character* that nurture true happiness and well-being. These are the positive qualities that, when used to influence and inform simple, everyday decisions, can have a profoundly positive effect on our own lives, and the lives of those around us.

Character is strengthened by the choices you make: the small, daily decisions to think, speak, and act in a way that reflects the best of who you are *now* and shapes the best possible version of who you will *become*.

A Little Pebble of Kindness

Ever thrown a pebble into a lake? The pebble sinks immediately, but its effect can be seen long after the small rock disappears. Little waves ripple out across the surface, tiny at first, but growing larger, spreading out across the water. For something as small as a pebble, the effect is much greater than expected.

The things we do and say are often similar to pebbles thrown into the water. Their effects can be great.

Something as simple as a kind word, a smile, or a friendly gesture could have a lasting impact.

A little "pebble" of kindness may be the catalyst to inspire, motivate, and encourage someone in ways you never imagined. Long after they forget what you said or did, they will remember how you made them *feel*.

The Impact of Attitude

Attitudes are strange things. They're not very complicated; after all, there are only two kinds: good and bad. But as simple as they are, attitudes can have the most significant impact on our lives and the lives of others.

Our attitude influences the way we perceive situations, feel about people, frame issues, react to life's challenges, hear what is said, and interact with others.

A positive attitude provides a clear set of lenses through which we view the world. It is one of confidence and optimism. It promotes a sense of well-being, a sense of hope and happiness. It encourages us to be and do our best.

A negative attitude provides a blurry lens through which we view the world. It is one of self-doubt and pessimism. Negativity casts a shadow of dissatisfaction and unhappiness over life.

Because our attitude determines how we interact with others, it can also have a direct impact on those around us. Attitude, in other words, can be contagious. The attitude we choose to have will spread to those around us. Will your impact be positive or negative?

Voluntary Followship

It's said that some leaders are born, and others are made. Regardless of the cause or path to leadership, a leader is ultimately granted the right to lead by the followers. The true test of leadership is *voluntary followship*.

The leader-follower relationship is one of mutual respect. The leader who has earned *voluntary followship* has taken the time to convey a clear sense of purpose to the follower and given the support needed to fulfill that purpose. A leader who respects the follower understands the needs of the follower. In turn, the follower willingly and confidently follows the leader giving the leader the full benefit and respect of the position.

Without mutual respect the leader-follower relationship is nothing more than one of compliance.

When a leader leads in such a way as to earn the respect of the follower, the relationship not only becomes mutually productive, it becomes inspirational; it unites both the leader and the follower in a meaningful relationship and helps *both* achieve greatness.

Great Leadership Inspires

We're all tempted to think of a leader as someone who seems to exude power and strength - someone with natural, effortless confidence. We may even be tempted to consider success a leadership quality. But while these qualities are often found in leaders, are they the qualities that make a leader great? Not necessarily. If strength, power, and confidence were the only characteristics of a great leader, the schoolyard bully would qualify.

No, strength, power, confidence, success, and even other qualities such as charisma and charm, are not the key marks of great leadership.

Great leadership *inspires*.

A great leader inspires others to be great. A great leader has the ability to bring the best out in others, while helping them pursue and achieve their personal goals.

A great leader motivates others into action.

A great leader inspires others to become what they were meant to be, what they were created to be, and to find their purpose in life.

Treat People as the Person They Can Become

Life is a journey, a work in progress. Every day each of us is becoming all that we are capable of becoming - at different paces.

Not everyone has reached their full potential. Some of us need help getting there. Each of us can have an impact - positively or negatively - on helping other people reach their full potential.

Do you recall who that person was that helped *you* become who you are today?

Perhaps they helped you see possibilities when all you could see were problems. Perhaps they had faith in you when you were doubting yourself. Perhaps they recognized a talent that you did not know you had. Perhaps they encouraged you to think of bigger possibilities.

Try seeing someone for what they can become. Choose to help someone unleash their greatness!

Questions to Consider

1. Are you being a source of joy to others?

2. How are you paying forward your gratitude to those who helped you get where you are today?

3. Have you brought out the best in someone today? Have you helped them unleash their greatness?

About the Author

Carl F. Hicks, Jr., consults with successful senior executives and business owners who want more. More personal and professional growth. More productivity and profitability. More meaning and happiness. More quality thinking time.

As President/CEO of The Growth Group, LLC, Carl works with some of America's best-managed companies helping them to identify and develop their top managerial talent, strengthen their work teams, and optimize their organization's performance.

Through his conversational-coaching approach, Carl keeps clients actively engaged and focused on critical strategic initiatives, growth, and profitability - while maintaining a balance between their *Life Style Goals* and their *Livelihood Goals*.

Clients range from emerging entrepreneurs to Fortune 100 firms. His results-oriented approach to management combines a formal management education—Ph.D. in Business Administration and MBA from The University of Arkansas and B.S. in Management with Distinction from Mississippi State University — with more than thirty years of practical consulting experience.

Carl is on the **Board of Directors** of Lifetime Financial Growth, LLC, serves as a **Strategic Advisor** for Butler Snow Advisory Services, LLC, and has been recognized by Birkman International as a **Senior Birkman Consultant**, a designation earned by only 5% of their consultants worldwide.

Carl and his wife, Carolyn, have a daughter, Natalya, and son-in-law, Mahmoud, who have blessed them with three wonderful grandchildren. Carl and Carolyn share their homes in Chevy Chase, Maryland and Hilton Head Island, South Carolina with Delta, their beloved Maltese.

Visit TheHicksFix.com today!

Learn more about our unique services:

- **Understanding My Motivational Drivers™ Report**
  Discover what makes you *click*, and how you can share this valuable information with others.

- **Executive Coaching**
  Expand your scope of possibilities, eliminate perceptual constraints, and journey to your next level of success.

- **Team Strengthening**
  Increase the productivity and profitability of your organization by maximizing your team's effectiveness.

- **Organizational Optimization**
  Align your strategy, structure, staffing, and systems in a way that propels your organization where you want it to go.

- **Subscribe to Monthly High Impact Ideas**

Carl F. Hicks, Jr., President/CEO
The Growth Group, LLC
5425 Wisconsin Ave Suite 600
Chevy Chase, MD 20815
240-351-4897
CarlHicks@TheHicksFix.com